100
YEARS OF
DERRY

The city of Derry, in the 1990s, is developing into a modern European centre for industry, commerce and culture. ROY HAMILTON

100 YEARS OF DERRY

ROY HAMILTON

THE
BLACKSTAFF
PRESS

BELFAST

Abbreviations

MAGEE	University of Ulster, Magee College
NLI	National Library of Ireland
NMGNI	National Museums and Galleries of Northern Ireland
UFTM	Ulster Folk and Transport Museum
WAG	W.A. Green Collection
WELB	Western Education and Library Board

First published in 1999 by
The Blackstaff Press Limited
Blackstaff House, Wildflower Way, Apollo Road
Belfast BT12 6TA, Northern Ireland

© Roy Hamilton, 1999
All rights reserved

Designed by Della Varilly Design

Printed in Ireland by Betaprint

A CIP catalogue record for this book
is available from the British Library

ISBN 0-85640-661-9

For Mum, Marion, Peter, Mark, Audrey and Adam

Acknowledgements

I would like to thank the following people for their help in the compilation of this book. To Colm Arbuckle, Susan Brown, Jimmy Cadden, William Carson, Billy Coulter, Phil Coulter, Maura Craig, Bishop Edward Daly, Michael Doherty, Richard Doherty, Larry Doherty, the Donaghey family, Willie Duffy, Charles Friel, Daphne Gallick, Charlie Glenn, Dana, Ken Goodall, Ken Goodman, Paddy-Ann Griffith, George Haire, Declan Hasson, John Hume, Roy Johnston, Dorothy Laird, Charles Logue, William Loughlin, William Lynn, Dorothy Magowan, Ken Martin, Nonie McCormick, Gay McIntyre, Eamonn Melaugh, Donna McStravick, Brian Mitchell, Sam Mitchell, John Magowan, Don O'Doherty, Don J. O'Doherty, Dan O'Connell, Margaret O'Hara, Patsy O'Kane, Billy Platt, Will Pomeroy, Tommy Shiels, Billy Sinclair, Dick Sinclair, Gary Sloan, Albert Smallwoods, Mina Ussher, Jim Wallace and Tim Webster. To David Bigger and Terry McDonald, for access to their marvellous collection of photographs of Derry, a very special word of thanks.

I am grateful to the National Library of Ireland for giving permission to use photographs from the Lawrence Collection, the trustees of the NMGNI Ulster Folk and Transport Museum for the use of photographs from the Green Collection, to the University of Ulster, Benburb Priory, the Central Library of the Western Education and Library Board, Foyle and Londonderry College, the Memorial Hall Museum, the Diocesan Library, Foyle Valley Railway Museum, the *Londonderry Sentinel*, Thornhill College, St Columb's College, the *Derry Journal*, Derry City Council, the Londonderry Port and Harbour Commissioners, Planning Office DOE (NI) and the Sisters of Mercy for use of their archival material, and to BKS Surveys, BBC, Carlisle Road Methodist Church, Du Pont (UK) Limited, St Columb's Cathedral and the Londonderry Naturalists' Field Club for use of their photographs, and to all those who took the trouble to help me find the images which have made this publication possible.

A very special word of thanks to Janet Lundy and Roddy Hegarty for providing an oasis when times were dry and arid, and to Carina Rourke for her energy and attention to detail.

Contents

The River Foyle meandering down towards the lough with Binevenagh mountain on the right and Moville and Shrove in Donegal on the left. The Foyle and Craigavon bridges can be seen as well as the old walled city, one mile in circumference. Derry's population today stands at an estimated 106,000. BKS SURVEYS

Introduction

The city of Derry, which stands on a hill overlooking the River Foyle, was established as a monastic settlement in early Christian Ireland. The monastery was founded in or near an oak grove or wood by Colmcille (Columba) around AD 546 and was thus named Doire Cholmcille (the oak grove of the dove of the church) in honour of its founder. The settlement thrived until the sixteenth century, when English expeditionary forces arrived and left the religious foundations in ruins. From this period on, there were increased attempts to bring Ulster under the influence of an anglicised central government and by 1609, under the direction of James I, a plantation scheme had been devised that would see the creation of a new settlement by the English and Scottish in Ulster. In 1613 a development corporation of the city of London, the Irish Society, was set up to manage the plantation in County Coleraine (later County Londonderry).

The Irish Society laid out the foundations of Derry as we now know it: the historic city walls and four fortified gates were built between 1613 and 1618, as were the four principal streets which, although renamed – Shipquay Street was originally Silver Street, Bishop Street was Queen's Street, Ferryquay Street was Gracious Street and Butcher Street was the Shambles – still make up the distinctive cruciform shape which meets at the Diamond. At this time, also, because of the London connection, the city was renamed Londonderry. The Irish Society also managed the construction of St Columb's Cathedral, a magnificent specimen of Ulster architecture known as Planter's Gothic. Completed in 1633, it is one of the most important seventeenth-century buildings in Ireland and to this day serves as the cathedral of the Church of Ireland diocese of Derry and Raphoe.

The seventeenth century saw a heightening of religious tensions in Europe and Ireland, and these were to erupt spectacularly in Derry. With James II on the English throne, trying to re-establish Catholic authority throughout his kingdom, the measures undertaken in Ireland (placing Catholics in positions of power) brought the situation to a head. Plans were laid to bring William of Orange (a Protestant) from Holland to establish himself on the English throne. William, married to James's daughter Mary, arrived in Ireland to do battle with James and from this followed the Siege of Derry in 1688–9 which began when the city gates were closed by a group of apprentice boys attempting to defend the city against a Catholic invasion. For 105 days the city withstood the besiegers before relief ships

The Siege of Derry, 1688–9. This engraving hangs in St Columb's Cathedral, and in the image the artist has depicted a series of incidents which would have occurred over a number of days.
ST COLUMB'S CATHEDRAL

broke through the Jacobite barricades, across the River Foyle, bringing the siege to an end. This event continues to have an enduring symbolic value for Protestants in the city and throughout Northern Ireland, and is commemorated every year in the Apprentice Boys march of 12 August, the date which marked the end of the siege. It was also as a result of the siege that Derry was named the Maiden City, a testament to the fact that its walls have never been breached.

The eighteenth century was a time of economic growth and development for the city, especially in the linen trade, but it was not until the late nineteenth century that Derry really began to thrive. This century marked the industrial heyday of the city and saw the establishment of its key industries, the most significant and sustained of these being shirt-making. William Scott, a Derryman, is credited with having founded the industry in the 1850s, but it is thanks to a group of Scottish businessmen – Peter McIntyre, Adam Hogg, William Tillie and John Henderson – that the now familiar red-brick shirt factories were built, and that the industry really took off. Shirt-making was to serve Derry well for almost 150 years, providing work mainly for the women of the city, and a sense of pride in a product which received acclaim around the world.

It was also at this time that the banks, which underpinned Derry's business life, were established. The buildings themselves had an impressively rich architectural style. Strong frontages with Corinthian columns of polished marble led to lavishly furnished interiors, and many had Italianate balconies from which the managers could survey the commercial life of the city, especially in one of the main thoroughfares, Shipquay Street. Equally wishing to impress the local businessmen, the Commercial Buildings in Foyle Street, from where trade was conducted around the world, also had Corinthian columns, but lacking the riches of the bankers, their columns were made of polished granite.

Derry's industrial growth was substantially aided by the fact that the city was a port and could easily establish trade and passenger routes. By 1836 there were regular sailings to Glasgow and Liverpool, and later to Morecambe and Fleetwood. Derry was also a major emigration port and became a central departure point for the thousands who left Ireland in the nineteenth and twentieth centuries to seek their fortune in America and Canada. The companies of J. and J. Cooke and William McCorkell, in particular, played a major role in this 'trade' – their ships set off with a cargo of emigrants and returned with timber and grain from America.

As a port, the shipbuilding industry was also to play a significant part in Derry's economy, particularly in the late nineteenth and early twentieth centuries. The year 1830 saw the first patent slip dock constructed under a contract placed with Pitt Skipton and Company, and although this business failed, it led, in 1847, to Captain William Coppin, a Derryman, establishing his own yard which remained open until 1870. Charles F. Bigger, also a local man, successfully revived the business in 1886 and by the early 1900s over four hundred men were employed in his Derry yard. Not surprisingly, the industry drew workers from Scotland, particularly from Glasgow and the long-established yards of the Clyde, and their time in the city is still remembered through the street names – Glasgow Terrace, Argyle Terrace, Argyle Street and Glasgow Street.

Although distilling, both legal and illegal, had been associated with Derry for many years, it was only in the nineteenth century that it became established as an important part of the city's economy. By 1830 there were distilleries at Pennyburn, Waterside and Abbey Street. David Watt, the son of local merchant Alexander Watt, acquired both the Abbey Street and Waterside distilleries in 1839 and 1870 respectively and they went on to become hugely successful. By 1887 the Abbey Street complex, now the biggest distillery in Ireland and one of the biggest in the United Kingdom, was employing at least two hundred men. The Abbey Street distillery became famous for its Tyrconnel grain whiskey and the Waterside distillery for its Inishowen malt whiskey. Both distilleries closed in 1920.

The Watt family lived on Culmore Road and, going down river, their house – now a part of Thornhill College – was the third after Boom Hall, which was originally built by the Alexanders and was owned by the McDevitt family until the mid-1970s. The second house was Brooke Hall, owned originally by Sir George Hill before being bought by the Gilliland family. The three houses were visible from the river and the Derry sense of humour, always to the fore, is well demonstrated by the story, often told as emigrants travelled to Moville, in County Donegal, to set sail for America. The joke goes that someone on board one of the small boats would always call out 'You're now passing Boom Hall', then, a little later, 'And this is Brooke Hall', and finally, as the boat passed the Watt's house, a voice would shout 'And this is Alcohol'.

By the 1900s the city had no fewer than four railway lines. The Great Northern Railway (GNR), which evolved from the Londonderry and Enniskillen Railway, had, by 1847, a link between Derry and Strabane and by 1854 the line was extended to Enniskillen. By 1937 it had connections to Dublin, the journey lasting three hours and fifty-five minutes. The city was linked to Belfast by the Belfast Northern Counties Company (later the Northern Counties Committee) from the Waterside station of the London, Midland and Scottish (LMS) company. The Donegal Railway, operating from Victoria Road, was a narrow-gauge railway that ran along the east bank of the Foyle. It served places such as Cullion, Donemana and Ballymagorry, before reaching Strabane. The fourth railway, the Londonderry and Lough Swilly, ran mostly into north Donegal. Known locally as the 'Buncrana train', its terminus was behind the Custom House, beside the Guildhall, and it

Clearing snow from the line in the 1900s. MAGEE D282

served stations at Bridgend, Burnfoot and Buncrana, eventually extending as far as Carndonagh. Unlike the other lines to the east of the city, the Donegal lines remained under local control, giving the city a virtual monopoly on trade with its neighbouring county.

The first bridge across the Foyle (a wooden one), linking the Waterside (on the east bank) to the Cityside, was built in 1790, to be replaced in 1863 by the Carlisle Bridge, named after the lord lieutenant of Ireland, the Earl of Carlisle.

With an effective communications network and a thriving economy based on industry and trade, Derry entered the twentieth century a prosperous and enterprising city. Its population had just passed the forty thousand mark, making it the fourth largest city in Ireland, and causing it to expand beyond its seventeenth-century boundaries. The growing population spread up Creggan Hill towards Rosemount, where yet another shirt factory had opened in 1904, and northwards along the Foyle. It also began to sprawl onto the east bank of the river on the Waterside as more and more people moved to the city from the surrounding countryside as well as from counties Tyrone and Donegal. The railways, which carried goods to and from the port, also carried people towards the ever-growing city in search of work.

Derry now had a buoyant trade in shirts, whiskey and, of course, people and became the main market centre for the north-west, creating employment opportunities in the various foundries, tanneries, cooperages as well as the tobacco and fish-processing industries. By 1902 there were more than thirty shirt factories scattered across the city and surrounding districts, employing about eighteen thousand people, mostly women. Clusters of working-class communities, made up of labourers and factory workers, sprang up around the periphery of the city.

Derry's educational needs were, by the turn of the twentieth century, being served by not only a number of national elementary schools but notably by two grammar schools. Foyle College, built in 1814 and standing on Lawrence Hill, was the successor of the Free School built in 1617 as a result of money donated by Matthias Springham, one of two commissioners appointed by the Irish Society. It stood roughly where St Augustine's Church is today. St Columb's College was

Magee College, clearly visible at the top of the photograph, with, in the foreground, Strand Road and the River Foyle. BIGGER/ MCDONALD COLLECTION

opened in 1879, taking day scholars and boarders to prepare them for Maynooth and other ecclesiastical colleges, and later for civil service examinations. These colleges would be followed, in time, by what eventually became known as Londonderry High School and by Thornhill College, which extended grammar school education to girls in Derry. The city also had Magee College, opened in 1865 and named after its benefactor, Martha Magee, wife of a Presbyterian minister. Its initial function was to prepare men for the Presbyterian ministry.

In spite of such resources, education remained, by and large, the preserve of the better-off in society and for most was limited to the few years of primary education that could be acquired at the national schools. What opportunities did exist were often as a result of the initiatives taken by the respective church authorities who saw education and social improvement as running hand in hand. Not until the Education Act of 1947 would the working-class community have any real chance of a grammar school education. The act would also prove particularly important for the Catholic population and would play a key role in the growth of a Catholic middle class. In the meantime, much of the employment that was available to school leavers was in the form of unskilled and semi-skilled labour.

The opening years of the twentieth century, although still industrious and productive, also saw depression and unemployment cast their shadows over Derry. The industries which had thrived during the second half of the nineteenth century were starting to decline as a result of increasing competition from new suppliers and new material. The city also had a series of setbacks around this time, the most significant being the damage of important buildings, civic and commercial, due to fire. During this period Austin's department store and the Guildhall suffered severe damage and the town hall, then located in the Diamond, was completely destroyed. Although Austin's was rebuilt and continued to grow in stature and the Guildhall was restored and given a new lease of life, Derry was still unable to compete commercially with Belfast, nor was it able to generate the large-scale industry which could have supplied jobs for the male population.

Some respite arrived in the lead up to the First World War (1914–18) when the shipbuilding industry was temporarily resurrected, the local yard having been taken over by the Tyneside company of Swan and Hunter in 1912. The shirt factories too received a boost, supplying shirts for the forces. A more widespread

The shirt industry – for over 150 years the economic life blood of the city. MAGEE C073

The band of the 10th Royal Inniskilling Fusiliers (Derry Volunteers), taken before departure to France in 1915 as part of the 36th (Ulster) Division. A large percentage of the band were members of Derry's Hamilton Band, and in action they worked as stretcher bearers. At the Battle of the Somme, 1 July 1916, 22 officers and 742 other ranks went 'over the top'. Only 10 officers and 336 other ranks emerged unscathed. GARDINER MITCHELL

form of employment was the war itself. Against the background of the home rule crisis, large numbers of Protestant men enlisted in the 36th (Ulster) Division. Drawn mainly from the Ulster Volunteer Force, which had been set up in 1913 to defend Ulster against home rule, these men saw the war as a means of affirming their connection with Britain and the empire. However, by now Derry was largely a Catholic city and the men from this community were divided in their attitude towards the war. The Catholic clergy, led by Bishop Charles McHugh, encouraged their flock to support the war effort and consequently many joined the 16th (Irish) Division.

Though the First World War, to some extent, subsumed religious and political tensions, the sense of unity was to be short-lived. The tensions and divisions which had always bedevilled the city returned with the signing of the Anglo-Irish Treaty and the creation of the new Northern Ireland state in 1921. This left the growing Catholic population marooned within a predominantly Protestant state. The alienation felt by the Catholic community in Derry was exacerbated by the manipulation of the electoral system which effectively guaranteed unionist control of Londonderry Corporation. Over the course of the next few years tensions would increase, probably fuelled by continued gerrymandering and the economic depression of the post-war years – Watt's distillery closed in 1920, followed by the Swan and Hunter yard, one of the few sources of male employment, four years later. With unemployment at almost 30 per cent by the mid-1920s, an estimated three thousand people would emigrate before 1936.

After the First World War, which saw great strides in the development of the sea plane, Derry became the base for the Royal Air Force's flying boat facilities on the Foyle. The planes, wooden-hulled Supermarine Southamptons, were used for anti-marine exercises and long-range reconnaissance work. Wonderful air displays were also run by people like Alan Cobham and C.W.A. Scott. As well as the air displays, people could take flights over the city, giving them their first opportunity to see Derry from the air.

Irrespective of political developments, the city's infrastructure continued to develop, with a bus service being established in 1921. Partition, at first, did not affect trade with neighbouring Donegal, and on market days the city thronged with people who had travelled from across the border. The town was particularly busy in May and December when the Rabble Days or the annual hiring fair took place. Even up until the late thirties, Rabble Days continued to be held in the Diamond and were an opportunity for farmers to hire domestic servants and labourers. This period also saw the growth of public forms of entertainment. The Opera House which stood in Carlisle Road, although established in the 1880s, was particularly popular around this time. The cinema too became a popular leisure activity in this period and by 1934 Derry had six cinemas, amongst them the Palace in Shipquay Street, the Midland in Bond's Hill in the Waterside, the City Cinema in William Street and the Strand picture house, which exists to this day.

Except for occasional high points, such as the Eucharistic Congress of 1932 or the unscheduled arrival of Amelia Earhart, the first woman to fly solo across the Atlantic, in the same year, the 1930s were a relatively quiet period in Derry's history. In 1933 the city was used as a refuelling depot for a transatlantic flying boat 'armada' led by General Italo Balbo, who was en route to a Centennial Exhibition in Chicago. The armada had been sent by Italian dictator Benito Mussolini, who had decided to let the world see the pride of his government, the Italian Air Force. The Derry stop was made into a festive occasion, with General Balbo and his pilots being entertained by Mayor Sir Dudley McCorkell and the citizens of Derry, especially the Italian families who had settled there. Derry's Italian community was made of people who had come here for economic reasons, and the names of Yanarelli, Battisti, Fiorentini, Macari, Delpinto, Cafolla, Cassoni, Marchini and Corriea became synonymous with ice-cream parlours and tea and coffee rooms, situated in Strand Road, Ferryquay Street, Carlisle Road, William Street and Duke Street. Their ice-cream was much sought after and it was a common sight to see queues outside their shops, especially on sunny, summer Sunday afternoons.

There was also a Jewish community in the city, who had fled Nazi Germany to set up their businesses. With names such as Epstein, Lazarus, Szilagg, Sckuler,

Spain, Gordon, Sechules, Frieslander and Fredman, they made their livings as bedding manufacturers, toy-makers, moneylenders and makers of ladies' handbags. Frederick Szilagg had a small shirt factory, and Mrs Sechules made 'dress roses' at her premises in Carlisle Road.

The fact that Derry is a border town meant that smuggling was endemic in the 1930s. For many people it became a way of life and hundreds of yarns have entered the local folklore. Stories about the movement of tobacco, tea, butter, sugar and eggs from the southern side to Derry homes are told with relish. The railways were the obvious route, but there's many's the tale told of walking from Buncrana to Derry, using as many back roads as possible. For the bolder and more adventurous, the main road past the two customs' posts was the way to go.

Galliagh customs post, Buncrana Road, November 1939, with B Specials on guard. BIGGER/MCDONALD COLLECTION

The 1930s saw the emergence of pork 'factories', where pigs were slaughtered, ham and bacon cured, and the meat sold on to butchers' shops. Situated mostly in the Foyle Street, Duke Street and Bishop Street areas, the names of William Grant, John Logue, Buchanan Brothers, Roulstone and McLaughlin, James Mitchell, Macdonald Brothers, and Bigger's were well known in the city. For generations, pig-rearing had been one way of adding to the family budget and providing a 'wee roughness of money', as the Derry idiom would have it. Many of these pigs were kept in back yards and in August and December they would be taken to the factories. The animals would have been fed on what is known locally as 'brock', a mixture of vegetable peelings and general kitchen leftovers. The brock would have been collected door to door in small hand-drawn carts, mostly by young boys. When the time came to take the pigs to the factories, it was usually the women of the house who undertook this task, the belief being that if the menfolk were entrusted with the job, the money would have spent on drink on the way home.

Political differences, of course, continued to generate much debate, both locally and in the Northern Ireland parliament at Stormont. The greatest bone of contention at this juncture was the decision, in 1936, by the Stormont parliament to oversee changes to the electoral divisions within Derry. These changes effectively manufactured a permanent majority on the corporation for the unionist minority. In spite of rising discontent, violent conflict did not erupt.

On the economic front the city remained hushed. The problem of high unemployment persisted but the outbreak of war in 1939 again brought new work opportunities. For the local population the war offered a means of regenerating the economy and an opportunity to shelve old animosities in the face of a common enemy. Its real impact, however, was felt on 15 April 1941, when a German bomber, attempting to destroy the docks area, dropped two parachute mines. One exploded in Messines Park, killing fifteen people and injuring as many again; the other landed at Pennyburn and damaged a Catholic church.

Servicemen and technicians from Canada and the United States of America arrived in their thousands during the war years, the first of them – a group of 362 technicians – in June 1941. By February 1942 the United States had commissioned a naval base on the River Foyle. The base, which cost $70 million, housed some 150 patrol vessels that were used to guard the convoys which formed a life line between western Europe and the US in the lead up to the Normandy invasions. A British base, HMS *Ferret,* was also established on the Foyle and became an important anti-submarine training centre. The Royal Air Force established two airfields near the city, at Eglinton and Maydown, and the latter supported the largest operational squadron of the Fleet Air Arm in Britain. Maydown was also loaned to the Royal Navy and was commissioned as HMS *Shrike* – twenty thousand seamen were said to be based in the city during the war years.

After the depressed interwar years the arrival of American and Canadian servicemen, and the luxury goods they brought with them, caused great excitement for the people of Derry. The first port of call for many Americans after leaving the

American entertainer Frances Langford being tutored by a piper of the 'Irish Marines'. Influenced by their surroundings and their Irish-American adjutant, Major James J. Dugan, the Marine Battalion Drum and Bugle Corps took bagpipe lessons and formed a pipe band. The battalion also adopted a shamrock arm badge. Eleanor Roosevelt visited the city and the marines at Beech Hill House. BEECH HILL HOTEL

United States, the city got to hear first-hand about the latest dance crazes, and songs performed by such greats as Frank Sinatra were being enjoyed here long before they hit the high spots of Europe. The result of these foreign influences was felt particularly in the dance halls – the 'Mem', the Memorial Hall on the corner of Magazine Street, the 'Crit', the Criterion Hotel in Foyle Street, and the Corinthian in Bishop Street. Many of the local men, however, saw the American and Canadian servicemen as competition, not for jobs but for women. Their fears were well-founded – a large number of Derry women found a partner from overseas during these years, and although some remained in Derry, many left for a new life in America.

The 1950s began on an optimistic note. A mood of celebration swept through Britain and Northern Ireland with the coronation of Queen Elizabeth II in 1953, and the city played host to her in that same year as part of her coronation tour. Derry also saw the construction of much-needed housing in developments like the Creggan estate on the Cityside and Irish Street on the Waterside. New job opportunities were created with the establishment of the Birmingham Sound Reproducers (BSR) plant at Bligh's Lane, manufacturing record players. In 1957 the American chemical company, E.I. Du Pont de Nemours, announced its plans to build a plant for the manufacture of synthetic rubber at Maydown, on the site of the former naval aerodrome, HMS *Shrike,* a few miles outside the city. Production began in 1960 and since then the plant has gone from strength to strength. At present investment in the site amounts to £1,000 million, with an annual return of £70 million to the economy of the north-west.

Beneath the prosperity, however, religious and political tensions simmered. In spite of forming an obvious minority in the city, the unionist population had continued to maintain control of Londonderry Corporation since the Stormont intervention of 1936. A growing campaign throughout the north had captured the imagination of many from within the Catholic community who felt themselves to have been disenfranchised by the unionist authorities. The result was the Northern Ireland Civil Rights Association (NICRA), founded in February 1967. The organisation campaigned for an end to gerrymandering and for the introduction of a system of 'one man one vote' in local elections. Having successfully established itself in mid-Ulster during the early part of the year, its influence spread to Derry. On 5 October 1968 NICRA organised a march to draw attention to housing discrimination against Catholics within the city. The march was deeply controversial, and the behaviour of both the government – who had banned the march – and the police – who were accused of brutality – was condemned in the official report of the Cameron Commission in 1969. Amongst those involved in the march was a young John Hume who, within months, would replace Eddie McAteer, the sitting Nationalist MP for Foyle.

Pressure continued to mount and a new student-led organisation called the People's Democracy organised a march from Belfast to Derry in January 1969. Demonstrators were attacked by loyalist protesters at Burntollet outside the city and again as they entered Duke Street on the Waterside. As with the march of the previous year, a large number of marchers were severely beaten and they accused the local police of collusion with loyalists. Tensions simmered over the next six months with sporadic outbreaks of rioting and a number of demonstrations were banned. The annual Apprentice Boys parade on 12 August saw clashes between Catholic youths and police spiral out of control and led to three days of fierce rioting which became known as the Battle of the Bogside. It was this violence which, on 14 August, resulted in the deployment of troops in Derry where they were to remain for the next three decades.

Unfortunately the arrival of troops did not end strife. Catholic support for the army, which had initially been high, was severely damaged when two locals were killed by soldiers in July 1971. Dissatisfaction grew as clashes between the police or army and locals became more commonplace and recruitment to the recently formed Provisional IRA increased. The dam burst on Sunday, 30 January 1972, when a civil rights march, which had been banned, proceeded to make its way from the Creggan estate towards the city centre and the Guildhall. What exactly happened remains the subject of heated debate but within a few minutes of the deployment of the 1st Battalion of the Parachute Regiment thirteen unarmed demonstrators had been killed and another fatally wounded. The events of these few minutes and their aftermath were to be etched in the memory of the city and beyond and became known as Bloody Sunday.

As a result of Bloody Sunday, and the ever-increasing violence which followed, Derry became a microcosm of the Troubles in Northern Ireland. The commercial heart of the city was virtually destroyed by an unrelenting bombing campaign and the Guildhall was severely damaged in June 1972. By the beginning of the 1980s one in ten of the buildings in the city centre had been reduced to a state of dereliction. The situation was further worsened by the hunger strikes of 1981 which claimed the lives of ten republican prisoners, two of whom were natives of Derry. Their deaths, funerals and the violent protest which resulted from them, set in motion another cycle of violence which would continue well into the following year. Bombs, shootings, rioting and protests all became a familiar way of life once again.

The 1980s, however, also saw the tide begin to turn for Derry with a series of

Josef Locke, one of Derry's most famous sons. Born Joe McLaughlin in Creggan Street in 1912, he later joined the Royal Ulster Constabulary, where he was known as the 'Singing Bobbie'. During the Second World War he served with the Irish Guards in North Africa, and he became a professional singer when the war ended, his ballads and dreamy lullabies bringing him widespread popularity and success. And simply nobody performed 'Hear my Song' like him. He died in October 1999. MICHAEL DOHERTY

developments and investments which would increase self-confidence and promote a more positive self-image. The Inner City Trust, a cross-community body established in 1981, has played a crucial role in regenerating Derry both economically and culturally, and in attracting new businesses and industries to the city. New shopping developments at Lisnagelvin and Ballmagroarty, as well as the flagship development within the old city, the Richmond Centre, have made a substantial improvement to Derry's commercial profile. Of particular importance has been the setting up of Derry Boston Ventures, an organisation designed to establish links between the north-west and the east coast of America. The organisation's most significant achievement to date has been in obtaining investment from the Boston-based development company, O'Connell Brothers, to build the massive Foyleside shopping centre, which opened in 1995.

Culturally, the 1980s also proved to be a vibrant and stimulating period for the city. In 1984, for example, Magee College found a new lease of life as a campus for the University of Ulster and by 1997 the numbers of students had risen from one hundred to almost three thousand – at last the city had the university which had been denied it in the 1960s. The Orchard Gallery, which had opened in 1978, forged an international reputation for itself as a centre for the visual arts. The establishment of the Field Day Theatre Company in 1980, which included such illustrious figures as Seamus Heaney, Stephen Rea, Tom Paulin and David Hammond, and of the Foyle Film Festival in 1987 provided important injections of self-confidence into the city. They also contributed to the development of one of Derry's most thriving industries – tourism.

The last twenty years have seen an influx of visitors to Derry, due in part to a harbour enhancement scheme at Lisahally which brought cruise ships to the port. These visitors have led to the development of hotels, pubs and other tourist-oriented services. In promoting itself as a tourist location, Derry has drawn on its own rich history and has used it as a catalyst for current economic and cultural redevelopment. The Foyle Valley Railway Museum and the Harbour Museum, for example, draw on the city's industrial heritage and maritime history respectively, while the Tower Museum and the Workhouse Museum and Library explore the social, political and religious history of the city. Exhibition galleries, too, are emerging as witnessed by the Heritage Library and the Orchard Gallery. The Genealogy Centre, opened in 1981, and the Heritage Centre, opened in 1997, have also made important contributions to Derry's thriving tourist industry.

One reason for the city's popularity as a tourist destination is its reputation for music and the arts. Derry shot to fame in 1970 when a young girl from the city called Rosemary Brown won the Eurovision Song Contest for Ireland. Better known to millions as Dana, her song 'All Kinds of Everything' provided a glimmer of hope at the height of the Troubles. Along with her, Josef Locke, Phil Coulter and the Undertones are just some of the singers and entertainers who have helped to put the city on the map. Derry also has a rich literary reputation – Brian Friel, the playwright, comes from the city, while Nobel Prize-winner Seamus Heaney was born in County Derry and like Seamus Deane, who is a native of the city, attended St Columb's. Deane's 1996 novel, *Reading in the Dark,* set in Derry, was short-listed for the Booker Prize. The opening of the Verbal Arts Centre in 1992 has also helped to cement Derry's literary and cultural reputation. The centre promotes media like literature, poetry and storytelling through public readings, community projects and other arts-related events.

Derry has also received a number of other boosts, mainly as a result of new businesses and industries investing in the city. In the 1980s the American firm, Fruit of the Loom, opened two large plants just outside the city, while new computer-based businesses brought in by Seagate Technology, which opened in 1995, and Stream International, which opened in 1997, effectively pulled the city in from the periphery of Europe into the hub of the information technology era. In spite of this, unemployment continues to pose a problem for Derry. The last few years, for

The O'Doherty Tower, rising above the seventeenth-century walls. KEN MARTIN

15

example, have seen the closure of one of the Fruit of the Loom plants and of the car manufacturers, United Technologies, both resulting in heavy job losses.

As the city looks towards the twenty-first century and the celebration of the new millennium it continues in its efforts to come to terms with its economic problems and with the darker elements of its history. For this reason, the visit of the President of the United States, Bill Clinton, and his wife Hillary, in November 1995, some fifteen months after the announcement of the first IRA ceasefire, was deeply symbolic. For many it was seen as a watershed, the opening of a new chapter in the city's history. The millennium celebrations which Derry City Council have planned hope to sustain this positive momentum. At East Wall construction is well underway on the Millennium Complex, a cultural centre which will contain a new one-thousand-seater auditorium and theatre. The council has also unveiled ambitious plans to match this cultural development with the creation of new job opportunities and the provision of training that can sustain the new industries which they hope to attract. More broadly, it is hoped that the millennium celebrations can be used to build bridges between Catholics and Protestants in the city. To this end Derry's millennium festival will be centred on the River Foyle. So often viewed as the physical divide between the Waterside and the Cityside, between nationalist Derry and unionist Londonderry, the river, it is envisaged, can also act as a healing, uniting confluence as this city and its people enter the third millennium.

Roy Hamilton
Derry
August 1999

1900s

The Sinclair children, *c.* 1901, left to right: Dick, Mary and Tommy. Their father Archibald was born in Scotland in 1862 and was a tin-plate worker. He came to Derry in the 1890s to make biscuit tins for Brewster's bakery. It's interesting to note the large water butt on the right of the photograph with the wooden tap at the bottom because at that time their house in Hawthorn Terrace would have had no running water. Judging from their costumes, they obviously had vivid imaginations when it came to dressing up. SINCLAIR FAMILY

On 28 July 1903 King Edward VII, Queen Alexandra and Princess Victoria arrived in Derry. They had sailed into Buncrana aboard HMS *Victoria and Albert*, and travelled on to Derry on the royal steam locomotive *Edward VII*. MAGEE D351

Having travelled by carriage up Shipquay Street and through the Diamond, passing the Corporation Hall (later destroyed by fire in 1907), they moved through Ferryquay Street and down Carlisle Road. The road is bedecked with flags in honour of the occasion. The entourage continued past the newly erected Carlisle Road Methodist Church, which can be seen on the right with scaffolding still on its spire, and the Opera House. The group then travelled, via John Street and Foyle Street, to the Guildhall, where they lunched with the mayor, Alderman Marshall Tillie. MAGEE B154

G SIDE. DERRY. 5377. W L

Overview of the Bogside from the tower of St Columb's Cathedral, *c.* 1900. Walker's Pillar can be seen, the chimneys of Watt's distillery and St Eugene's Cathedral. The Apprentice Boys Memorial Hall on the right is the original building dating from 1873. NLI, LAWRENCE C5377

Looking down through Crawford Square with its terrace of three-storied houses, developed between the late 1850s and the 1870s, the clock tower of the asylum is visible. The asylum's foundation stone was laid on 11 May 1827 by Bishop William Knox and the first patients were admitted in 1829. On the River Foyle the sailing ships are at anchor in the busy port and, looking across the river, Ebrington Barracks, laid out in 1839, can be seen. The square is still lit by gaslight. NLI, LAWRENCE R2881

Laying the foundation stone of Carlisle Road Methodist Church, 1901. The ceremony was performed by the Duchess of Abercorn, with Sir Faudel Phillips, the governor of the Irish Society, in attendance. The opening service took place on 8 May 1903 when the church's minister, the Reverend George R. Wedgewood, presented Mayor Marshall Tillie with a gold key, which he used to unlock the door and declare the church open for public service.
CARLISLE ROAD METHODIST CHURCH

Bishop Street, looking down towards the Diamond and the Corporation Hall, is filled with
people celebrating the Relief of Derry (12 August). On the immediate right is the courthouse
and on the left is the Church of Ireland's bishop's palace. Further down on the right is the
deanery and in the far distance, to the left of the Corporation Hall, the spire of the
Guildhall is visible. NLI, LAWRENCE R3364

The Great Northern Railway terminus from Carlisle Bridge. Building work began in 1845 and was completed in 1847. Here horsepower is literally being used to shunt the rolling stock. The wooden wharf running along the river front was removed in the early 1920s.
BENBURB PRIORY

Looking across the River Foyle to the Derry side, c. 1900. The metal footbridge took passengers over the railway line to the ferry at Ebrington Barracks, which then sailed to Harbour Square. This is a busy river scene with many sailing ships lined along Queen's Quay. NLI, LAWRENCE R2876

Watt's distillery was one of the largest distilleries in the United Kingdom. In its heyday it produced, at its Abbey Street site, 1,260,000 gallons of grain whiskey per annum and employed two hundred men. Here the famous Tyrconnel whiskey is being labelled and packaged. The distillery closed in 1920. MAGEE B295

William Graham's shop in the Diamond, c. 1900. The shop stood in the corner between Austin's and Bishop Street, and the large sign above the window displays, 'London Pianoforte Warehouse', doesn't quite tell the whole story as the shop also sold sheet music and tuned pianofortes as well as selling them. NLI, LAWRENCE R6202

Austin's department store under construction, c. 1909. Standing in the Diamond at the corner of Ferryquay Street, the skeleton of the now familiar dome towers over the scene. The first building on the site was established in 1830, but in 1907 it was destroyed by fire and sparks from it set the nearby Corporation Hall alight. The shop proudly claims to be 'the first purpose built store in Ireland'. AUSTIN'S

This turn-of-the-century photograph shows a group of scholarly young gentlemen at St Columb's College looking very serious and dressed in severe clothes. The college was opened at the casino built by Frederick Augustus Hervey, Anglican bishop of Derry and 4th Earl of Bristol, in the late eighteenth century.
ST COLUMB'S COLLEGE

City of Derry Boating Club, 1907, winners of the Lady Elizabeth Cairns, Portadown News, and City of Derry Grand Challenge Cups. The club took part in regattas and races, some of them on the River Foyle, starting from the boathouse at Boating Club Lane. MEMORIAL HALL MUSEUM

Boys from St Columb's College taking part in a game of cricket, not a sport normally associated with the college. St Columb's College

Londonderry High School was established in 1928 and was the amalgamation of two girls' schools, Victoria High School and St Lurach's College. This photograph, *c.* 1915, shows a hockey team from Victoria College, which was situated in Crawford Square. Foyle and Londonderry College

The foundation stone for the Guildhall in Shipquay Place was laid in 1887, and the building was gutted by fire on Easter Sunday, 1908. This photograph, taken shortly after the fire, shows the fire brigade still in attendance and a crowd of sightseers surveying the scene. In the right foreground is a circular building known as the Iron Man – the toilets.
MAGEE B563

30

The Guildhall was rebuilt after the 1908 fire. Here hoardings surround the building, and as is the case even today, they are being used by local traders to advertise their merchandise.

BENBURB PRIORY

1910s

Shipquay Street in 1910 – a busy commercial thoroughfare. At the foot of the street the Guildhall is still being rebuilt, with scaffolding clinging to the spire and the clock face still to be installed. Notice the hand cart packed at ninety degrees on the left-hand side of the street. CENTRAL LIBRARY, WELB

The Diamond in 1912. At that time the Diamond was laid out in ornamental gardens, after the demolition of the town hall in 1910. The statue of Sir Robert Ferguson, elected MP for Derry in 1830 and who held the seat for thirty years, at the top of Shipquay Street was moved in 1928 and now stands in Brooke Park. Austin's department store stands proudly on the corner of Ferryquay Street, and a lending library, Pickett's jeweller's and Austin's Medical Hall fill the opposite corner. NMGNI UFTM, WAG 99

The Ulster Volunteer Force, raised to provide unionists with a means to resist home rule, came into being in January 1913. The force quickly grew in numbers and by 1914 it was 100,000 strong. The 2nd Battalion City of Derry Regiment had their base in Hawkin Street, and are seen here, c. 1915, displaying guns and bandoliers. BIGGER/McDONALD COLLECTION

The Irish Volunteers were formed at a meeting in the Rotunda in Dublin in November 1913. Here a unit has gathered for a drill session in Celtic Park on the Lone Moor Road in 1914. The cap badge, with its harp insignia, indicates an officer status in the force. MAGEE C741

Andrew, Hugh, Thomas and John Sinclair from Hawthorn Terrace. Five brothers served in
the forces during the First World War, and these four lost their lives. Because of this tragedy,
the fifth brother, Dick, was brought to England and did home service for the remainder of
the war. SINCLAIR FAMILY

A group photograph taken in the grounds of Bayview House on Asylum Road. Mayor Robert Newton Anderson is seated centre front, and to his left are the Duchess of Abercorn, president of the Londonderry War Hospital Supply Depot, and Mayoress Anderson. BIGGER/ MCDONALD COLLECTION

The Great Hall of the Guildhall, richly decorated and with tables laid for a celebratory meal. Seated in the hall are servicemen and servicewomen, with their spouses, being entertained on their return from the First World War. MEMORIAL HALL MUSEUM

In the early 1900s shipbuilding was an important provider of jobs. The North of Ireland Shipbuilding Company was an offshoot of the Tyneside company of Swan and Hunter. The Londonderry Port and Harbour Commissioners pledged they would do everything they could to help establish a large industry in Derry. One major source of trade for them was the construction of steamships for the Canadian Great Lakes. This photograph, taken outside the offices of the company, shows guests at the launch of the *Ville D'Arras* in September 1917. HARBOUR COMMISSIONERS

Carlisle Bridge, opened on 25 September 1863, was 1,180 feet long and 30 feet wide and was actually narrower than its predecessor, the wooden bridge. It was said to be the most beautiful structure of its kind in the United Kingdom. The tramway on the lower floor connected the quays and railways on both sides of the river to facilitate the increasing trade of the city. The arrangements for lighting the bridge were of the fairest kind – half the lamps were supplied from the Cityside, and the rest from the Waterside gasworks. At the base of each lamp was a shield, with the city arms. BENBURB PRIORY

City Factory, 1919. In the 1850s and 1860s shirt factories operated without electricity. Especially in the cutting department, the workers relied on natural light. The cutting area, with its templates for different styles and long tables for laying out the cloth, was on the top storey of the factory, where the roof was constructed of large panes of glass. Here the shirt began its journey. The cloth was cut and then began to make its way down through the different departments until the finished product arrived on the ground floor to be boxed and taken to the nearby docks for export. MAGEE C080

City Factory, 1919. After cutting, the next stage is sewing. It is reported that when shirt-maker William Tillie arrived in Derry from Scotland, he had a sewing machine under his arm. Magee C072

City Factory, 1919. One of the last jobs was in the smoothing department, where the finished shirts were ironed before being packaged. The irons were heated by gas taken from overhead pipes via a rubber hose. Magee C077

MEMORIAL HALL. WALKER'S PILLAR. 2558. W.L.

Walker's Pillar. During the Siege of Derry, 1688–9, the Reverend George Walker, Church of Ireland rector of Donoughmore, was joint governor of the city. The first stone for the pillar was laid on 7 December 1826 by Mayor Richard Young and the work was completed by 1828, costing £4,200, including £100 for the statue. Governor George Walker's likeness was taken from a painting in the possession of one of his descendants. The pillar was destroyed by a bomb in 1973. In the left foreground is the Apprentice Boys Memorial Hall. NLI, LAWRENCE 2558

Christchurch, situated on Infirmary Road, opposite St Eugene's Cathedral. The Church of Ireland church was built in 1830 under the auspices of Bishop William Knox. Transepts and a chancel were added in 1881, and it was damaged by fire in 1996. It has since been restored and was rehallowed by Dr James Mehaffey, bishop of Derry and Raphoe, on 1 May 1998, in the presence of Archbishop Robin Eames. CENTRAL LIBRARY, WELB

1920s

Carlisle Road. This beautifully atmospheric photograph shows a typical 1920s day in Derry, with (left) prams being pushed along the street in front of the Provision Store, the window cleaner's ladders outside Gordons, and (right) the message boy's bicycle propped against the pole and a forerunner to the public phone box, a shop that invites you to use their own phone. BIGGER/McDONALD COLLECTION

Waterloo Place in the late 1920s, where horses and carts are now competing with cars and lorries. The 'golden teapot' of McCullagh's grocery shop can be seen on the left. BIGGER/
MCDONALD COLLECTION

Right: this photograph, taken by Baxter Robinson, a press photographer who worked for the *Londonderry Sentinal* and the *Derry Standard*, shows a female ice-cream vendor on the quays during a regatta day in the city. CENTRAL LIBRARY, WELB

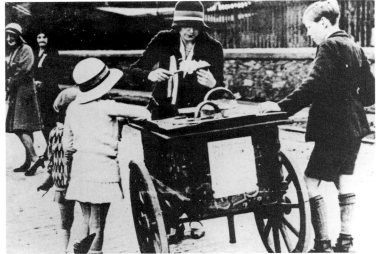

Below: Cuthbert Street in the Waterside, 12 August 1922, with its elaborate arch celebrating the Siege of Derry (1688–9) and the Battle of the Boyne (1690). JOHNSTON FAMILY

The launch of the SS *New York News*, the last ship launched by the North of Ireland Shipbuilding Company in May 1922. The company had a brief boom during the years of the First World War but the depression dealt a final blow to shipbuilding in Derry and the yard closed in 1924. HARBOUR COMMISSIONERS

City of Derry Rugby Football Club 1st XV, winners of the North-West League, 1927–8.
Teams from Coleraine, Limavady, Derry, Strabane and Enniskillen competed in the league.
The president of the club, Bishop Irvine Peacocke, is seated centre front. CITY OF DERRY RUGBY
FOOTBALL CLUB

Clooney Rovers Football Club was one of the best junior teams in the North-West League, right up to the 1980s. CENTRAL LIBRARY, WELB

McMonagle's Long Car, 1929, at its terminus on Strand Road, beside the Bryce and Weston shirt factory. This service operated until 1931. One of H.M.S. Catherwood's buses is also in shot, another famous name in Derry's transport history. Bigger/McDonald Collection

The Palace Cinema, Shipquay Street, 1929, where an enormous new loudspeaker is just
about to be offloaded. However, the first 'talkie' shown in the city, *The Jazz Singer*, was in the
Midland Cinema in the Waterside. BIGGER/McDONALD COLLECTION

The Britannia Band, 1925. The band started off as a flute band in 1866, changed to brass in 1875, and finally added reeds some years later. BRITANNIA BAND

The Ulster Special Constabulary, the B Specials, was established in October 1920 as an auxiliary police force to the Royal Irish Constabulary. It remained in being until 31 March 1970, when it was replaced by the Ulster Defence Regiment. Photographed here is Culmore Company B Special Constabulary, on the occasion of the governor general's state visit to Derry in 1928. In the front row three officers wearing medals are veterans of the First World War. MEMORIAL HALL MUSEUM

The hockey team from the Convent of Mercy in Pump Street, before the establishment of Thornhill College. THORNHILL COLLEGE

The home of the Watt family, owners of Derry's famous distillery. The house was bought by the Sisters of Mercy in 1929 and was opened in 1932 as Thornhill College. THORNHILL COLLEGE

Wreath-laying at the War Memorial in the Diamond, *c.* 1928. The occasion is the anniversary of the Battle of the Somme, 1 July 1916, and the girls are wearing their dead fathers' medals.
BIGGER/MCDONALD COLLECTION

This poignant emigration scene of a young family about to set out for a whole new life is taken on board a paddle steamer just before it sailed down the Foyle for Moville in County Donegal. It is estimated that between 1926 and 1936 some three thousand men from Derry 'took the boat' and emigrated. BIGGER/MCDONALD COLLECTION

1930s

The sad young face of emigration. CENTRAL LIBRARY, WELB

The Anchor Line offices in Foyle Street, often the first port of call for Derry people preparing to take the emigration route. BIGGER/MCDONALD COLLECTION

From the happy expressions on these people's faces, it doesn't look as if they are about to set sail as emigrants. They are probably taking part in a boat drill on board one of the liners. Bigger/McDonald Collection

The paddle steamer *Seamore* taking passengers down to the emigration ships anchored at Moville in County Donegal. On Saturday evenings, Sundays and most public holidays the tenders were used as pleasure cruisers to take daytrippers to Moville, with a band playing on board. Bigger/McDonald Collection

The opening of Craigavon Bridge by the lord mayor of London, Sir Percy W. Greenaway, 18 July 1933. Also in attendance are Mayor Sir Dudley McCorkell, Town Clerk Sir F. Henry Miller, Alderman Captain James M. Wilton, and Prime Minister Lord Craigavon. BIGGER/McDONALD COLLECTION

Craigavon Bridge under construction. Named after Lord Craigavon (the first prime minister of Northern Ireland) the new bridge, like its predecessor the Carlisle Bridge, had the unusual distinction of having two decks. It was opened in 1933. CENTRAL LIBRARY, WELB

Construction gang for the rebuilding of the Model School, 1936. The original school was opened on 25 September 1862 by the lord lieutenant of Ireland, the Earl of Carlisle, on the same day he opened and gave his name to the Carlisle Bridge – the first iron bridge across the River Foyle. WILLIE DUFFY

A hiring fair – 'the rabble' – in the Diamond in 1937. Until the late 1930s local farmers would come to annual hiring fairs to inspect and hire labourers and domestic servants. Young boys and girls would sign on for six months' work, some as young as twelve. The wages were poor, the working hours long, and living conditions appalling, but for many it was the only means of making a living. BIGGER/McDONALD COLLECTION

Carlisle Road and the funeral of fireman McGowan, where crowds have gathered to watch the cortège go past. The fire engine is flanked by serving officers and the horse-drawn hearse can be seen in the background. The Welch Margetson shirt factory, opened in 1876, is in the left foreground. BIGGER/MCDONALD COLLECTION

Two extremes – the internal combustion engine and the horse-drawn van – show how the Rock Biscuit Company delivered their wares. Well-turned-out servers, complete with white coats and caps, sit proudly on their respective conveyances. On this occasion they are on their way to a parade in the Brandywell showgrounds. BIGGER/ MCDONALD COLLECTION

Back to the horse – or in this instance the pony and trap. William Goligher (on the right) sits proudly behind the reins. The man standing on the road could be a soldier from Ebrington Barracks, possibly laying the trail for the Garrison drag hunt. HAMILTON FAMILY

A Brewster's bread van, *c.* 1932, with Tom Kee (right). Bread servers called at homes daily, bringing a range of Brewster's products right to the doorstep. USSHER FAMILY

In the 1930s goose was often a part of the Christmas dinner. The geese were reared in the country in villages like Park. The locals 'walked' the geese to Derry to be put on the 'Scotch' boat, and it took three days to complete the journey, stopping overnight in fields where the geese could feed and rest up. Michael McElhinney from Park recalls the noises and the smells of those journeys. To prepare for the marathon, he says, the geese were walked first through soft tar and then over dry sand, putting layers of tar and sand on their feet, 'shoes' almost. Once in Scotland, they were bought by farmers and fattened by farmers' wives for the Christmas market. LONDONDERRY SENTINEL

The city's Girl Guide movement had its origins in the early 1920s. Here the company is preparing for a church parade.

LONDONDERRY SENTINEL

Derry's first scouting patrol met at Sunbeam Terrace in 1908. Here we see a 1930s scout leaders' training group at Culmore. Seated, second left, is the Reverend H.A. McKegney, whose name is synonymous with scouting in the city. Minister at St Augustine's, he served the movement at all levels throughout his life.

LONDONDERRY SENTINEL

First Derry Boys' Brigade on parade in the Guildhall, being inspected by Major Mosse of the 2nd Battalion the Leicestershire Regiment, and standing to his left J.J. Hill, captain of the company. The Boys' Brigade had a strong presence in Derry and whereas the scout movement tended to concentrate more on outdoor activities such as camping and hiking, the Boys' Brigade tended toward athletic displays and parades. LONDONDERRY SENTINEL

June 1932 saw Dublin as the venue for the Eucharistic Congress. Thousands flocked there and Derry's Catholic Boy Scouts of Ireland were no exception. Here the troop and its leaders are being given a tremendous send-off at the Great Northern Railway terminus on Foyle Road. BIGGER/MCDONALD COLLECTION

Gywn's Institute, Brooke Park. John Gwyn was born near Muff in County Donegal, and moved to Derry to start a grocery business in Bishop Street. In his will he left a large sum of money to be used for the education of orphan boys. The money went towards the building of the institute, completed in 1840. A later bequest by James Young enabled girls to benefit. It was destroyed by an IRA bomb in 1973. These young rascals look as if it wouldn't take much for them to be up to mischief. The nineteenth-century smooth-bore canon is of at least ten-inch calibre and was probably a spoil of war or part of the equipment of the old Londonderry Artillery Militia. How it found its way to Brooke Park remains a mystery.
BIGGER/MCDONALD COLLECTION

Outdoor markets were very much a part of the city's street scenes. Bargains were struck here and deals agreed there with a slap of the hand and a handshake, not of course forgetting the luck's penny. Poultry are for sale here and the poster on St Columb's Hall announces a forthcoming Charlie Chaplin film. The three men huddled against the back wall could well be discussing a terribly secretive deal.

BIGGER/McDONALD COLLECTION

The Derry firm of James Harper Limited, boot and shoe manufacturers, traded in Duke Street in the Waterside.

BIGGER/McDONALD COLLECTION

Right: Jimmy 'Spider' Kelly, winner of the British and Empire Featherweight titles in 1938 when he defeated Benny Caplin at the King's Hall, Belfast, in November. DERRY JOURNAL

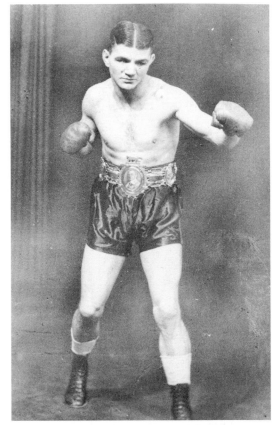

Below: Prehen Golf Club, with an enthusiastic crowd following the fortunes of Dr A.L. Weir (left) and W.G. Robertson. The club was opened in 1912 as a nine-hole course and in the early 1930s an eighteen-hole course was completed, the par being struck by the Golf Union of Ireland in 1932 as seventy-four. LONDONDERRY SENTINEL

E.D.R. Shearer played for Derry City in the 1930s. He was also an international cricketer, was the first north-west cricketer to be capped for Ireland, and the first to score a century in a North-West Senior Cup Final. He still holds the record individual score of 233 runs in north-west cricket. HENRY MILLAR

GNR football team, 1926–7. A youthful Jimmy Kelly is seated second right. He went on to play for Derry City Football Club from 1930 until his last game in 1951. LONDONDERRY SENTINEL

Right: a service at the city's War Memorial in the Diamond, the wreath being laid by the lord mayor of London. MAGEE B939

Opposite: in 1932 Amelia Earhart became the first woman to fly solo across the Atlantic. She left Harbor Grace in Newfoundland on 20 May and landed on 21 May at Ballyarnett, near Culmore. The flight lasted just over thirteen hours and she made the journey in a bright red Lockheed Vega, now on display in the Smithsonian Museum, Washington DC. She had intended to fly to Paris but had navigational problems. She saw the River Foyle, followed it inland, and landed in a field known locally as Cornshells. Working there was a James McGeady, and when Earhart asked him where she was, he promptly replied 'Cornshells' – which meant nothing to her. Her next question reputedly was 'Do you know anywhere where I could wash my hair?'
CENTRAL LIBRARY, WELB

Boys from St Columb's College, followed by Convent of Mercy girls, returning to school down Bishop Street after attending a Mass in St Eugene's Cathedral during the Eucharistic Congress. Patrick Grant's shop is still there today, having been passed down to Patrick's son Harry and then to Harry's son Philip – the present owner. ST COLUMB'S COLLEGE

One of the many Eucharistic Congress arches erected in the city during June 1932, when the congress was being held in Dublin. At a celebration open-air Mass in the Phoenix Park, Count John McCormack sang live on Radio Éireann. Wirelesses were brought out into the sunny streets around Rossville Street, Lecky Road and Fahan Street, all bedecked with flags and bunting in the colours of the congress – royal blue and gold – and the papal colours of yellow and white, and the air was filled with the strains of 'Panis Angelicus'. BIGGER/McDONALD COLLECTION

Above: in 1933 Benito Mussolini sent his air minister, General Italo Balbo, on a propaganda armada on behalf of his fascist government. Seen here are a team of Italian meteorological experts, who were in Derry in 1932 to investigate the weather conditions that could be expected the following year.
LONDONDERRY SENTINEL

Above: Derry was home to a small community of Italian immigrants who in the 1930s formed themselves into a fascistii. On the wall behind this group can be seen a photograph of Benito Mussolini and, on the left and right, the King and Queen of Italy. BIGGER/MCDONALD COLLECTON

Opposite below: General Italo Balbo (centre) led the 'Balbada' of flying boats that had been sent, via various stopping-off points, on a propaganda trip to the Centennial Exhibition in Chicago. In all there were twenty-four boats, and they moored below Lisahally. He arrived in Derry in July 1933, and is seen here with city dignitaries and members of the local Italian community. BIGGER/MCDONALD COLLECTON

Competitors in the solo violin competition at Feis Dhoire Cholmcille: *left to right:* Maisie Strickland, Daniel McLaughlin, Terence McDonald and Patricia McDonald. In 1999 the feis celebrated its seventy-fifth anniversary, with some six thousand entrants.
BIGGER/MCDONALD COLLECTION

This quartet represented the city at a Royal Command Performance in the presence of King George V and Queen Mary in the Royal Albert Hall on Empire Day, 24 May 1935. Left to right: Jim Coyle (tenor), Nan O'Brien (soprano), Maud Laird (alto) and William Loughlin (bass). WILLIAM LOUGHLIN

The Apprentice Boys of Derry marching at Carlisle Square, 12 August Relief celebrations, c. 1935. MEMORIAL HALL MUSEUM

The 25th Battery of the 9th (Londonderry) Heavy Anti-Aircraft Regiment, Royal Artillery, on the move from Caw Camp to Larne, 4 November 1939. From Larne they travelled to Blackdown Camp in the south of England to prepare for overseas deployment, landing in Alexandria in Egypt on 27 November. BIGGER/MCDONDALD COLLECTION

1940s

A group of evacuees at the Model School, some with their mothers, before leaving by bus for dispersal centres in County Derry. Londonderry Sentinel

A collection of scrap metal gathered together by women from the Wapping Lane district of Derry. The scrap was melted down and used in the manufacture of planes, ships, guns and bullets.
LONDONDERRY SENTINEL

A cargo of four to five hundred tons of scrap metal being loaded for shipment on behalf of John Doherty and Son, Foyle Street. LONDONDERRY SENTINEL

Wartime civilian support. These nurses could be putting together 'comfort packs' for soldiers serving overseas. Comfort packs contained items such as socks, balaclavas, woollen gloves and non-perishable foodstuffs like boiled sweets – and sometimes cigarettes. LONDONDERRY SENTINEL

Residents of Argyle Terrace wearing gas masks, after being fitted out at Richmond Hall, with, on the left, Councillor R.J. Finlay, senior warden of District A2, and Miss V.E.M. Knox, deputy senior warden of District A3. LONDONDERRY SENTINEL

Belmont House, commandeered for war use. CENTRAL LIBRARY, WELB

Members of the Waterside Auxiliary Fire Service. Standing at the back, fourth from the right, is Frederick J. Simmons, the city's mayor throughout the war years, and to his left is John C. Donnell, the town clerk.

LONDONDERRY SENTINEL

Under the watchful eye of an interested, bemused observer, the 1st Battalion the 133rd Infantry Regiment of the us Army march up Duke Street on their way to Belmont Camp and Talbot Park, 26 January 1942. What was possibly bemusing him was the fact that he could not hear the marching feet. The US 'Doughboy' wore rubber-soled boots, but the British soldier was kitted out with leather-soled steel-tipped boots. The term 'Doughboy' comes from the dough cakes which were issued to American soldiers as part of their rations in the mid-nineteenth century.
CENTRAL LIBRARY, WELB

US marines arrive at the LMS terminus. Fifth from the right is Major James J. Dugan, adjutant and later commanding officer of the 'Irish Marines'.
BEECH HILL HOTEL

Photographed at the bottom of William Street, three US sailors are quickly coming to terms with the local weather. They would have arrived in the city on board a destroyer escort protecting an Atlantic convoy and would have had a five-day turnaround before going back to sea. RICHARD DOHERTY

Thoughts of home and riding the range are possibly uppermost in this US sailor's mind as he enjoys a trip on a donkey and cart. The American sailors became very popular in Derry, supplying the local children with candy and the women with silk stockings. At one stage 149 vessels were based in Derry, together with some 20,000 sailors. RICHARD DOHERTY

The Royal Navy jetty at Lisahally. Nine escort ships are docked, ready for their next operation in the Atlantic. <small>Central Library, WELB</small>

Colonel C.R. Shilstone, commander of the 3rd (Ulster) Anti-Aircraft Brigade, and the Duke of Abercorn, honorary colonel of the 9th (Londonderry) HAA Regiment, inspect the 25th Battery at Caw Camp. Four years to the day after this inspection, on 21 October 1943, fifteen of these men died when a German bomb fell on their gun pit at Villa Nuova in Naples. <small>Central Library, WELB</small>

German U-boat officers surrendering to Admiral Sir Max Horton, commander-in-chief of the Western Approaches, at Lisahally, 14 May 1945. Horton accepted the formal surrender at Lisahally to pay tribute to the vital strategic role that Derry had played in the final victory in the Battle of the Atlantic. Almost thirty German submarines eventually tied up at Lisahally and were later scuttled close to Rockall.

CENTRAL LIBRARY, WELB

Brigade Cricket Club, winners of the North-West Senior Cup in 1946. Cricket was first organised in the north-west by the County Derry Cricket Union, later known as the North-West of Ireland Cricket Union. The Senior Cup Competition was introduced in 1888 (Limavady won) and in 1894 the Senior League was formed with Sion Mills becoming the first champions. JIM WALLACE

Bowls have a popular following in the city. This green, at Brooke Park, was always kept in immaculate condition.
CENTRAL LIBRARY, WELB

The North-West Annual Senior Badminton Championship winners in the Guildhall, c. 1948. JIM WALLACE

St Eugene's Choir at Feis
Dhoire Cholmcille.
LONDONDERRY SENTINEL

Londonderry Feis, 1947. Jack
Wilkinson (left), from
Buncrana, won the Baritone
Advanced Class, and
Derryman William Loughlin
the Bass Advanced Class.
WILLIAM LOUGHLIN

St Columb's Cathedral Choir, 1948. Dean Lawrenson is seated in the middle of the first row with, on his right, the Reverend G.C. Willowby, and on his left the Reverend J.K. Kermode and Michael Franklyn, the choirmaster. ST COLUMB'S CATHEDRAL

The Londonderry Male Singers (originally known as the London, Midland and Scottish Singers) photographed behind the Guildhall after winning the male voice choir competition at Londonderry Feis. WILLIAM LOUGHLIN

4 January 1940: P.P. McMenamin, president of St Columb's College Union, presents
vestments to the Most Reverend Dr Neil Farren to mark his consecration as bishop of Derry.
ST COLUMB'S COLLEGE

1950s

Foyle Road residents, c. 1950. DONAGHEY FAMILY

Above: Fianna Fáil leader Eamon de Valera (first left) visited the city in 1951 to open a festival of Gaelic cultural and sporting events. CENTRAL LIBRARY, WELB

Opposite: Queen Elizabeth II, accompanied by Prince Philip, visited the city in 1953 as part of the queen's coronation tour of the United Kingdom. Shipquay Street is packed with well-wishers and the cavalcade of cars goes right back to Guildhall Square. CHARLES LOGUE

The one-coach 11.25 a.m. from
Strabane coasts into Foyle
Road on 26 June 1952.
N.W. SPRINKS

The Great Northern Railway
terminus, with the Belfast train
about to depart for Great
Victoria Street station. The
wagons in the foreground are
on the Port and Harbour
Commissioners' tramway.
CHARLES FRIEL

Everyday work in the pork stores. Fifteen male employees are preparing the meat in overcrowded, unhygenic working conditions. LAIRD FAMILY

Construction gang on the Creggan estate, *c.* 1950. Derry's postwar housing situation was chronic. However, the first new local authority houses in the Creggan estate were ready for occupation in 1947 and building continued into the 1950s.
CENTRAL LIBRARY, WELB

Birmingham Sound Reproducers (BSR) worker, *c.* 1952. In its heyday over two thousand workers, the majority of them male, worked in the BSR factory in Bligh's Lane, making record players and tape recorders. Dr Daniel McDonald opened his factory in 1952 and it closed in 1967. DAN O'DONNELL

A group of BSR press shop workers on their tea break. DAN O'DONNELL

A 1950s young man, proud of his new racing bicycle with dropped handlebars. Complete with the latest hairstyle, natty sports coat and shirt collar carefully arranged, he looks set to conquer the world.
DAN O'DONNELL

Londonderry High School, *c.* 1953, with a lone pupil entering by the back gate. In 1922 Victoria High School in Crawford Square and St Lurach's School on Lawrence Hill merged to become Londonderry High School. The home of shirt manufacturer William Tillie, at the top of what had been known as Tillie's Lane, was purchased and the school was established there in 1928. FOYLE AND LONDONDERRY COLLEGE

The old Foyle College on Lawrence Hill. Let your eye travel from left to right: first the small entrance to the bicycle shed, then the windows of the headmaster's study, next the staff entrance and to the far right the pupils' entrance. FOYLE AND LONDONDERRY COLLEGE

Londonderry Naturalists' Field Club in front of the Guildhall, about to set out on their annual outing. In 1998 the club celebrated its seventieth anniversary. LONDONDERRY NATURALISTS' FIELD CLUB

Thornhill College past pupils' reunion. Standing centre front is Dr Neil Farren, Catholic bishop of Derry. THORNHILL COLLEGE

Top Flight Stars of Variety was a series of concerts organised by Michael Kelly in the Guildhall in the 1950s. Entertainers such as Larry Parks, comedians Connie Stewart and Billy Livingstone and groups such as the Recordites played to packed audiences. The local talent included singer William Loughlin, and Pat and his Saddle Pals, a very early country and western band.
WILLIAM LOUGHLIN

The Melville Dance Band in the Corinthian Ballroom, Bishop Street. MELVILLE BAND

Men's hockey was popular in the north-west in the 1950s. The local YMCA club was a strong force, being able to field six teams per week, and it had the proud claim that it could field a team of interprovincial players in every position.
JOHNSTON FAMILY

Jimmy Delaney with the Irish Cup which Derry City won in May 1954 after a three-match marathon with Glentoran – drawing twice and winning the third 1–0. Born in Scotland in 1914, Jimmy Delaney played first for Glasgow Celtic, transferred to Manchester United in 1946 and later played for Aberdeen and Falkirk. He came to play for Derry City in January 1954. He is the only player to have won a Scottish cup medal (with Celtic), an English cup medal (with Manchester United) and an Irish cup medal (with Derry City). DERRY JOURNAL

Aerial photograph of the Strand Road area at the bottom of Lawrence Hill, showing the Municipal Technical College, now the Institute of Further and Higher Education, the old Foyle College, and the asylum. CENTRAL LIBRARY, WELB

Aerial view of St Columb's Cathedral, 1958. The cathedral was built between 1628 and 1633 and was the first Protestant post-Reformation cathedral built in the British Isles. It cost £4,000 and serves as both a parish church and the cathedral of the Church of Ireland diocese of Derry and Raphoe. Behind the cathedral Walker's Pillar can be seen and also the turrets of the Apprentice Boys Memorial Hall. MEMORIAL HALL MUSEUM

Bishop's Gate was rebuilt as a triumphal arch in 1789, on the centenary of the Siege of Derry. In this 1950s photograph the aptly named Arch Bar was still in existence and through the centre archway the former bishop's palace, now the Masonic Hall, is visible. MEMORIAL HALL MUSEUM

The *Laird's Loch* sailed between Derry and Glasgow carrying both livestock and passengers. Built for Burns and Laird in 1944 in Ardrossan, she was registered in Glasgow and ran from 1944 to 1966. She had 72,000 cubic feet of cargo space, forty-four saloon two-berth cabins and eight berths in steerage. SAM MITCHELL

Above: Altnagelvin Hospital. The foundation stone for the hospital was laid on 5 July 1956 by Lord Wakehurst, governor of Northern Ireland. The hospital opened for its first patient on 1 February 1960; it had 391 beds (it now has over 500) and cost £1.5 million. The hospital was officially opened by Lord Wakehurst on 1 July 1960. SAM MITCHELL

Right: statue of Princess Macha outside Altnagelvin Hospital. Princess Macha is said to have been the founder, in 300 BC, of the first hospital in Ireland at Eamain Macha (Navan Fort). The dove resting on her arm signifies Saint Colmcille (the dove of the church), who built a monastery which incorporated Derry's first infirmary in AD 546. The decoration includes oak leaves and acorns, a reference to Derry's Gaelic name Doire, meaning an 'oak grove'. SAM MITCHELL

1960s

Wintertime skating on Enagh lough. SAM MITCHELL

Carlisle Road, the main artery to the city centre, runs from Carlisle Square to Ferryquay Gate, seen here at the top of the street. This was the first gate that thirteen young apprentices closed to the troops of James II in December 1688 – the start of the Siege of Derry.
MAGEE B443

Above left: two stalwarts of the pantomine scene in the city, Don O'Doherty (left) and Mick McWilliams. DERRY DIOCESAN LIBRARY

Above right: pantomines were held in St Columb's Hall throughout the 1960s. Here Seamus McDevitt, a regular performer, is dressed for his part in *Babes in the Wood*. DERRY DIOCESAN LIBRARY

Right: Maureen Hegarty, principal girl in the 1965 production of *Babes in the Wood*. DERRY DIOCESAN LIBRARY

Four well-known faces on the local entertainment scene: Don O'Doherty on accordion, Leo McCaffery on fiddle, James MacCafferty at the piano, and his brother Don on double bass. They were part of a Taste of Ireland group from the city which annually toured the USA and Britain from 1963 to 1969. DON O'DOHERTY

The popular Gay McIntyre Orchestra, one of the earliest showbands in Ireland.
GAY McINTYRE

Billy 'Spider' Kelly, British and Empire Featherweight Champion, who made history by following in the footsteps of his illustrious father Jimmy, who had also been British and Empire Featherweight Champion – the first father and son ever to win British boxing titles. His career ended with an eight-round draw against Spike McCormick in the King's Hall in Belfast.

Derry Journal

The Irish Rugby team which toured Australia in 1967 at Áras an Uachtaráin, Phoenix Park, Dublin. Seated centre front is the president of Ireland, Eamon de Valera. The City of Derry Rugby Club is represented by Ken Goodall (back row, third right). Goodall has been described as the greatest Irish forward of the postwar age. He learned his rugby at Foyle College, went on to play for Ulster, and at the age of nineteen represented Ireland in his first international. In all he gained nineteen caps for Ireland between 1967 and 1970 before he was lost to the amateur game when he went to play rugby league for the English club Workington in 1970. KEN GOODALL

Above and right: Walker's Pillar. Until it was blown up in 1973, children considered it a great treat to go to the top of the pillar, with its superb view over the city and the Foyle.
SAM MITCHELL

Lecky Road, 'where the school played ball by the gas yard wall'. WILLIE CARSON COLLECTION

Mrs E.H. O'Doherty (second left), co-founder of Feis Dhoire Cholmcille, photographed with (from left) Dr James McCormick, Medical Officer for Buncrana, County Donegal, Charles McCormick, co-founder of the Derry Catholic Club, and Leo McCormick. McCORMICK FAMILY

The McLaughlin School of Dancers, one of the most successful dance schools in Derry. Opened in 1954, they are still going strong today. The school has produced many all-Ireland and Ulster champions, and currently in the city there are fifteen dance teachers who are ex-pupils. DON O'DOHERTY

Neighbourliness in Fountain
Place. Willie Carson Collection

Fountain Street, with
preparations under way for the
Twelfth celebrations.
WILLIE CARSON COLLECTION

Above: the east bank of the River Foyle, looking towards the Waterside. We see the neat rows of terraced houses running down to the boundary wall of the LMS terminus, where trains run to Coleraine and Belfast. The spire of St Columb's Church on Chapel Road is visible on the right and the large white building further right is Clooney Hall Methodist Church. SAM MITCHELL

Opposite: coal was imported into the port of Derry. Here it is being unloaded straight from the coal boat into Kelly's and Lane's lorries, two well-known local coal merchants. MAGEE B028

Foyle College moved from Lawrence Hill to new premises in Springtown in 1968. On 2 May the official opening ceremony was performed by the Duke and Duchess of Kent, seen here on the steps of the new building. FOYLE AND LONDONDERRY COLLEGE

Cardinal John D'Alton at the opening of St Mary's Church in Creggan. Bishop Neil Farren had conducted the dedication ceremony at the church on 31 May 1959. CENTRAL LIBRARY, WELB

Tillie and Henderson's shirt factory opened its doors on Foyle Road in 1857. The shirt factories were the major employers of female labour for many years. The building now stands derelict. MAGEE B071

The site for the Du Pont factory at the Maydown airfield. Built orignally to manufacture Neoprene, a synthetic rubber, first production was in 1960. It now makes two products, Kevlar® and Lycra®. DU PONT (UK) LIMITED

St Eugene's Catholic Cathedral, from Brooke Park. The church was built in 1873 and the spire was added in 1903. It takes its name from the founder of the ancient church of Ardstraw in County Tyrone, which subsequently evolved into the diocese of Derry. SAM MITCHELL

Rossville Flats under construction in 1965, built in an attempt to alleviate the chronic housing situation in Derry. High-rise flats were deemed a good idea in the 1960s, but many problems were not predicted and the flats were eventually demolished in 1992. Rossville Flats would soon be known worldwide with the start of the Troubles in 1969. SAM MITCHELL

Civil rights march, late 1960s. The Northern Ireland Civil Rights Association was formed in 1967, inspired by the civil rights campaign of Martin Luther King. It used a peaceful campaign of street protests and demonstrations to highlight discrimination. MAGEE C299

The Derry Citizens' Action Committee march of 16 November 1968, approaching police lines on the Cityside of Craigavon Bridge. The march, which included John Hume and Ivan Cooper, was banned from entering the Diamond by Bill Craig, the then minister for home affairs. LARRY DOHERTY

On New Year's Day 1969 a People's Democracy march set out from Belfast to Derry. On 4 January they were attacked by a crowd of loyalists at Burntollet Bridge, just outside Derry. BELFAST TELEGRAPH

The Battle of the Bogside, 12–14 August 1969. In protest at a 15,000-strong Apprentice Boys parade, intense rioting erupted between Catholics and the police. After three days and nights the police were completely overstretched and utterly exhausted. The British government called in the army, and on Thursday 14 August, at 5 p.m., eighty men of the Prince of Wales Own Regiment arrived in Derry. There was simultaneous rioting in Belfast, and the army were deployed there on 15 August. MAGEE B132

1970s

Civil rights leader John Hume attempts to defuel a potentially violent confrontation on the corner of Foyle Street and Shipquay Place. WILLIE CARSON COLLECTION

Bloody Sunday. On 30 January 1972 soldiers from the 1st Battalion the Parachute Regiment opened fire during a banned NICRA anti-internment rally, killing thirteen men (a fourteenth died later). Widespread horror and protest followed, as televisual images were shown throughout the world. The marchers were certain the troops fired first; the army said otherwise. The controversy continues nearly thirty years later, and a new government inquiry opened in Derry in 1998. MAGEE B136

Rioting at Free Derry Corner on Bloody Sunday. MAGEE B865

THE ARMY REGRET THE INCONVENIENCE CAUSED BY THESE CHECKS BUT HOPE YOU APPRECIATE THAT THEY ARE NECESSARY IN THE INTERESTS OF SECURITY.

The army regret. Strand Road, showing one of the many army checkpoints set up in the city during the 1970s. EAMONN MELAUGH

Shipquay Gate, where the army had established a checkpoint.
CENTRAL LIBRARY, WELB

Operation Motorman in Derry, 31 July 1972. At first light bulldozers and armoured personnel carriers were brought in to pull down barriers in the no-go areas of the Bogside and Creggan. During the operation, two people were killed in shooting incidents in the city.
LARRY DOHERTY

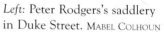

Opposite: bomb-damaged Strand Road close to Waterloo Place and opposite the old Victoria Barracks which was for many years the city's main police station. Among the buildings destroyed were the Embassy Ballroom and Foster's Tea Rooms. MAGEE C010

Left: Peter Rodgers's saddlery in Duke Street. MABEL COLHOUN

Duke Street, for many years the main street in the Waterside, leading to the LMS railway terminus. This little stretch of street was home to a disproportionate number of public houses. MABEL COLHOUN

137

Cityside. SAM MITCHELL

Waterside. Sam Mitchell

A young Rosemary Brown –
Dana – with her brothers in
the back garden of their home
in Creggan. BROWN FAMILY

On 26 March 1970 Dana won
the Eurovision Song Contest
for Ireland with 'All Kinds of
Everything'. BROWN FAMILY

Charlie Nash representing
Ireland at the 1972 Olympics
where Nash won both the
British and the European
Lightweight titles – the first
Irishman ever to do so. He was
also the first Derryman to fight
for a world title, when he was
stopped in the fourth round of
the fight by Jim Watt in the
Kelvin Hall, Glasgow, in April
1982. DONAGHEY FAMILY

The US Navy finally closed its gates in 1977 having been operating almost uninterruptedly in the city since 1942. The base was a vital link in the navy's worldwide communications network and from the early 1960s onwards it was a relay for the 'hot-line' between the White House and the Kremlin. MEMORIAL HALL MUSEUM

The killer whale 'Dopey Dick' who swam into the Foyle estuary and came upstream as far as the city in November 1977, the attraction for him, no doubt, being the fish for which the river is renowned. CENTRAL LIBRARY, WELB

By the 1970s McCullagh's 'golden teapot' had moved from Waterloo Place to the Waterside. MABEL COLHOUN

Brooke Park. When James Hood Brooke died in 1865 his will stated that he wanted the residue of his estate to secure an area of land to be used for recreation by the citizens of Derry. The money was placed in a trust fund and when his sister Margaret died in 1884 she also left the residue of her estate to the trustees. There was now a sum of over £10,000, which was used to buy land and design the park, and it opened in 1901. CENTRAL LIBRARY, WELB

The Gasworks, in the late 1970s, just before its closure. The gasworks opened in 1829 in Foyle Street and moved to this site in 1865. CENTRAL LIBRARY, WELB

The funeral of hunger-striker Patsy O'Hara. Aged twenty-three, he died in the Maze Prison on 21 May 1981, after sixty-one days on hunger strike. BELFAST TELEGRAPH

The new Foyle Bridge under construction. This section of the bridge had been floated on a large barge round the north coast from Belfast to Lough Foyle. Completed in 1984, it is the fourth bridge to span the river and is currently Ireland's longest. DONAGHEY FAMILY

The Foyle Bridge nearing completion and the central span has still to be installed. CENTRAL LIBRARY, WELB

Looking across Craigavon Bridge from the Waterside, the tower and spires of St Columb's, St Eugene's, Austin's and Carlisle Road Methodist Church dominate the skyline. CENTRAL LIBRARY, WELB

Above: First Derry Presbyterian Church. There has been a Presbyterian church and congregation here since *c.* 1642 although the main body of this building goes back to 1780 with restoration work being carried out in 1896, and the Roman Corinthian portico of red sandstone was added in 1903. ROY HAMILTON

Opposite: St Eugene's Cathedral from Westland Avenue, under major renovations. CENTRAL LIBRARY, WELB

Thiepval Memorial Accordian Band was founded in 1922. One of its most notable successes was in the 1984 all-Ireland band competition when it won the senior accordian section and the best overall performance. The band finally folded in 1996, and monies raised from the sale of the band hall and instruments were donated to St Columb's Cathedral and Christchurch. Seated here on Mayor John Tiernery's left is the band's conductor in the 1980s, Will Pomeroy. Thiepval Band

Hamilton Flute Band was founded in 1856. During the First World War the band is reported to have joined the 10th Inniskilling Fusiliers 'to a man', and became its regimental band.
Hamilton Band

Derry City, who in 1988 won all three competitions in the south's professional football leagues. In the early 1970s it had withdrawn from the northern Irish League, and after an absence of thirteen years a Derry City team began to compete in the southern League of Ireland in 1985. The 1988 team, under the management of Jim McLaughlin, included Felix Healey, later to become manager, and Liam Coyle and Paul Curran, who still play for the team. The present manager, Kevin Mahon, is seated first row, first right. Derry Journal

Stroke City's Gerry Anderson. He began his broadcasting career with BBC Radio Foyle in 1983, and soon had his own daily programme on BBC Radio Ulster. Here he's wearing a T-shirt advertising *The Show,* which he co-presented with Eamonn Holmes and Rhonda Paisley on BBC TV. In 1994 he spent some stormy months with Radio 4, but is now back on his home turf. BBC

Playwright Brian Friel (left) with actor Stephen Rea. The Field Day Theatre Company was founded in 1980, with Derry as its base. Its eminent board of directors includes Seamus Heaney, Seamus Deane, Tom Paulin, Brian Friel, Thomas Kilroy, Stephen Rea and David Hammond. CENTRAL LIBRARY, WELB

Since graduating from Queen's University Belfast in 1963, Derryman Phil Coulter has had a phenomenally successful songwriting career, from the Eurovision-winning 'Puppet on a String' to Derry's own anthem 'The Town I Loved So Well'. More recently he has also been an internationally popular performer and conductor. PHIL COULTER

A helicopter places a new cross on the spire of St Columb's Cathedral, August 1980. The anchor rod of the old cross had rusted away and the stonework had deteriorated badly. The replacement cross was carved from Leitrim sandstone, by a young sculptor from Scotland who had family links with Buncrana, on the ground floor of the cathedral schools, now the Verbal Arts Centre. MEMORIAL HALL MUSEUM

1990s

The Foyle Bridge. KEN MARTIN

The cruise ship *Seabourn Pride* anchored on the Foyle. When the cruise ship *Southern Cross* sailed into Derry in 1995 it was the first one for forty years. Passengers disembark and are given the opportunity to sample the hospitality, culture and heritage of the city and the surrounding area. DERRY CITY COUNCIL

The Foyleside Shopping Centre under construction. Built as part of a major regeneration scheme, it opened in 1995 at a cost of £65 million. PLANNING SERVICE DOE (NI)

Waterloo Place in the 1990s, the scene of so many bombings during the 1970s, is quite transformed today. ROY HAMILTON

Derry's Craft Village – a lovely tourist attraction with its shops, workshops, cafés and pubs. ROY HAMILTON

Sister Aloysius of the Sisters of Mercy, a gifted painter specialising in religious icons.
ROY HAMILTON

The main entrance to the original Sisters of Mercy Convent, St Peter's, Pump Street. The Sisters of Mercy arrived in Derry in July 1848, quickly establishing themselves and opening up a number of schools and their present convent, St Catherine's, is part of the original building. SISTERS OF MERCY

Dr James Mehaffey, Church of
Ireland bishop of Derry and
Raphoe, at St Columb's
Cathedral gates. ROY HAMILTON

Bloody Sunday mural, with Father (later Bishop) Edward Daly, capturing one of the most enduring images of the Troubles. Roy Hamilton

In the 1990s the Apprentice Boys of Derry organised pageants and re-enactments to commemorate the Siege of Derry and to help achieve a greater understanding of the background to the siege. In this late-twentieth-century version, the Williamite forces came from Sligo, and the Jacobite ranks were played by Derry men and women.
EAMONN MELAUGH

Loyalist mural in the Waterside. KEN MARTIN

In November 1995 US President Bill Clinton visited Northern Ireland – the first American president ever to do so. Derry was included in his itinerary. Photographed here at the Guildhall are, left to right: Lady Mayhew, Sir Patrick Mayhew, the then Secretary of State for Northern Ireland, First Lady Hillary Clinton, Mayor John Kerr, John Hume, Pat Hume and Mayoress Carita Kerr. NW FRAMES AND PHOTOS

The Hands of Friendship statue stands where Craigavon Bridge meets Carlisle Road. Unveiled in June 1992, it is the work of Derry sculptor Maurice Harron. SAM MITCHELL

In November 1998 SDLP leader, Derryman John Hume, was joint recepient, with Ulster Unionist Party leader David Trimble, of the Nobel Peace Prize. A. KNUDSEN

Forty-seven years ago John Magowan planted a tree on Sir Basil McFarland's estate, Aberfoyle. The tree was planted to commemorate the coronation of Queen Elizabeth II in 1953. John's father Sam was head gardener on the estate and the family lived in the gate lodge. Today the tree is alive and well and stands in the grounds of the Magee campus of the University of Ulster. In this 1953 photograph John is the young lad standing on the left proudly holding the tall spade. JOHN MAGOWAN

It's 1998 and John Magowan,
now the Local Development
Officer for Conservation
Volunteers Northern Ireland,
stands beside the oak tree that
he planted in 1953.
LONDONDERRY SENTINEL

Aerial view of the City of Derry Airport, which offers a range of services including direct flights to England and Scotland. Planning Service doe (ni)

The Londonderry Port and Harbour Commissioners moved from city centre docks to a new purpose-built dock and infrastructure at Lisahally in 1993. The move enabled the authorities to cater for a wider range of shipping and to provide more modern facilities for their customers. PLANNING SERVICE DOE (NI)

Hallowe'en is one of the
biggest nights of the year in
Derry, attracting visitors from
all over Ireland. Everyone dons
fancy dress, dances in the
streets, sings in the pubs. The
fireworks erupting over the
Foyle make a truly spectacular
sight. DERRY CITY COUNCIL

173

Bibliography

Bigger, David and Terence McDonald *In sunshine or in in shadow*, Friar's Bush Press, Belfast, 1990

Dallat, Cahal, *Altnagelvin, 30 glorious years: 200 years of medical care in Londonderry*, Shaun Grant at PMC Limited, 1990

Gallagher, Charles, *Acorns and oak leaves – a Derry childhood*, Dubh Regles Books, Derry, 1981

Galloway, Peter, *The cathedrals of Ireland*, IIS, Belfast, 1992

Gerard-Sharp, Lisa and Tim Perry, *Eyewitness travel guides: Ireland*, Dorling Kindersley, London, 1995

Hasson, Gerald, *Thunder and clatter: the history of shipbuilding in Derry*, Guildhall Press, Derry, 1997

Industries of the North one hundred years ago, Friar's Bush Press, Belfast, 1986

Lacy, Brian, *Siege city: the story of Derry and Londonderry*, Blackstaff Press, Belfast, 1990

Londonderry Teachers' Centre, *The shirt industry of the north-west of Ireland*, Derry

Milligan, Cecil Davis, *The walls of Derry: their building, defending and preserving*, Ulster Society, Portadown, 1996

Mitchell, Brian, *Derry a city invincible*, Grocer's Hall Press, Eglinton, 1990

Mitchell, Brian, *The making of Derry: an economic history*, Genealogy Centre of Derry, Derry, 1992

O'Doherty, Don, *City of Derry Golf Club*, Cityprint, Derry, 1987

Orr, David (ed.), *City of Derry Rugby Football Club Centenary, 1881–1981*, Nu Print, Derry, 1981

Our story so far ... St Mary's, Creggan ... 1959–1999, Cityprint, Derry, 1999

Rowan, Alistair, *North-west Ulster: the counties of Londonderry, Donegal, Fermanagh, and Tyrone*, Penguin, Harmonsworth, 1979